5701

TRAPPINGS

OTHER BOOKS BY RICHARD HOWARD

Poetry

Quantities, 1962
The Damages, 1967
Untitled Subjects, 1969
Findings, 1971
Two-Part Inventions, 1974
Fellow-Feelings, 1976
Misgivings, 1979
Lining Up, 1983
No Traveller, 1989
Like Most Revelations, 1994

Criticism

Alone with America, 1969
  (expanded edition 1980)
Preferences, 1974

TRAPPINGS

new poems

RICHARD HOWARD

turtle point press / new york

LIBRARY OF CONGRESS CATALOG NUMBER 98-061672
ISBN 1-885983-43-3

Text and cover design and composition by Melissa Ehn at
Wilsted & Taylor Publishing Services

FRONT COVER:
Dorothea Tanning, *Les cousins [The Cousins]*, 1970.
Courtesy of The Menil Collection, Houston.

Contents

for David Alexander

But I have that within . . .

TRAPPINGS

Dorothea Tanning's *Cousins*

synthetic fur over cotton stuffing,
wood base, 60 × 25 × 21 inches, 1970

She came to him in dreams, as he to her
in waking. And that was how they would meet,
ever wrong from the start, however right
               for the act, melting
together yet somehow sadly apart,
orifices certainly unmatched to
protuberances, although affording
               opportunity,
it appeared, in the oddest places; no
completion but the striving, the struggle,
the melancholy abandonment of his
               strain, her stratagem:
eventually, then, it came down to
this immense tedium, another name
for all our tenderness, solicitude.
               Ready and waiting,
but the hope forlorn, the motive foregone:
she tyrannically submissive to
his compliant despotism, he yielding
               over and underneath
to her surrender—her victory his
peculiar triumph. As if they neither
expected nor could resist, when it came,
               renunciation!
Their embrace, or—better—their lenient
enacting of what Milton himself calls

intimate impulse, has reached that
pitch of expertise
when the thing seen becomes the unseen thing.
With enemies like themselves (all *cousins*
"descended from a common ancestor"),
what lovers need friends?

Nikolaus Mardruz to His Master Ferdinand, Count of Tyrol, 1565

My Lord recalls Ferrara? How walls
rise out of water yet appear to recede
 identically
 into it, as if
built in both directions: soaring and sinking . . .
 Such mirroring was my first dismay—
       my next, having crossed
       the moat, was making
 out that, for all its grandeur, the great
pile, observed close to, is close to a ruin!
 (Even My Lord's most
 unstinting dowry
may not restore these wasted precincts to what
 their deteriorating state demands.)
      Queasy it made me,
      glancing first down there
 at swans in the moat apparently
feeding on their own doubled image, then up
 at the citadel,
 so high—or so deep,
and *everywhere* those carved effigies of
 men and women, monsters among them
       crowding the ramparts
       and seeming at home
 in the dingy water that somehow
held them up as if for our surveillance—ours?
 anyone's who looked!
 All that pretention

of marble display, the whole improbable
        menagerie with but one purpose:
                        having to be seen.
                    Such was the matter
            of Ferrara, and such the manner,
    when at last we met, of the Duke in greeting
        My Lordship's Envoy:
        life in fallen stone!

Several hours were to elapse, in the keeping
        of his lackeys, before the Envoy
                        of My Lord the Count
                        of Tyrol might see
            or even be seen to by His Grace
    the Duke of Ferrara, though from such neglect
        no *deliberate*
        slight need be inferred:
now that I have had an opportunity
        —have had, indeed, the obligation—
                        to fix on His Grace
                        that perlustration
            or power of scrutiny for which
(I believe) My Lord holds his Envoy's service
        in some favor still,
        I see that the Duke,
by his own lights or perhaps, more properly
        said, by his own *tenebrosity,*
                        could offer some excuse
                        for such cunctation . . .
        Appraising a set of cameos
just brought from Cairo by a Jew in his trust,
        His Grace had been rapt
        in connoisseurship,

that study which alone can distract him
from his wonted courtesy; he was
affability
itself, once his mind
could be deflected from mere *objects*.

At last I presented (with those documents
which in some detail
describe and define
the duties of both signators) the portrait
of your daughter the Countess,
observing the while
his countenance. No
fault was found with our contract, of which
each article had been so correctly framed
(if I may say so)
as to ascertain
a pre-nuptial alliance which must persuade
and please the most punctilious (and
impecunious)
of future husbands.
Principally, or (if I may be
allowed the amendment) perhaps Ducally,
His Grace acknowledged
himself *beguiled* by
Cranach's portrait of our young Countess, praising
the design, the hues, the glaze—the frame!
and appeared averse,
for a while, even
to letting the panel leave his hands!
Examining those same hands, I was convinced
that no matter what
the result of our

(at this point, promising) negotiations,
        your daughter's likeness must now remain
                "for good," as we say,
                among Ferrara's
        treasures, already one more trophy
in His Grace's multifarious *holdings,*
    like those marble busts
    lining the drawbridge,
like those weed-stained statues grinning up at us
        from the still moat, and—inside as well
                as out—those grotesque
                figures and faces
    fastened to the walls. So be it!

                                Real
bother (after all, one painting, for Cranach
    —*and* My Lord—need be
    no great forfeiture)
commenced only when the Duke himself led me
        out of the audience-chamber and
                laboriously
                (he is no longer
        a young man) to a secret penthouse
high on the battlements where he can indulge
    those despotic tastes
    he denominates,
        half smiling over the heartless words,
"the relative consolations of semblance."
                "Sir, suppose you draw
                that curtain," smiling
        in earnest now, and so I sought—
but what appeared a piece of drapery proved
    a painted deceit!

My embarrassment
afforded a cue for audible laughter,
    and only then His Grace, visibly
        relishing his trick,
        turned the thing around,
    whereupon appeared, on the reverse,
the late Duchess of Ferrara to the life!
    Instanter the Duke
    praised the portrait
so readily provided by one Pandolf—
    a monk by some profane article
        attached to the court,
        hence answerable
    for taking likenesses *as required*
in but a day's diligence, so it was claimed . . .
    Myself I find it
    but a mountebank's
proficiency—another chicane, like that
    illusive curtain, a waxwork sort
        of nature called forth:
        cold legerdemain!
    Though *extranea* such as the hares
(copulating!), the doves, and a full-blown rose
    were showily limned,
    I could not discern
aught to be loved in that countenance itself,
    likely to rival, much less to excel
        the life illumined
        in Cranach's image
    of *our* Countess, which His Grace had set
beside the dead woman's presentment. . . . And took,
    so evident was
    the supremacy,

no further pains to assert Fra Pandolf's skill.
        One last hard look, whereupon the Duke
                        resumed his discourse
                        in an altered tone,
        now some unintelligible rant
of *stooping*—His Grace chooses "never to stoop"
        when he makes reproof . . .
        My Lord will take this
as but a figure: not only is the Duke
        no longer young, his body is so
                        queerly misshapen
                        that even to *speak*
        of "not stooping" seems absurdity:
the creature *is* stooped, whether by cruel or
        impartial cause—say
        Time or the Tempter—
I shall not venture to hypothecate. Cause
        or no cause, it would appear he marked
                        some motive for his
                        "reproof," a mortal
        chastisement in fact inflicted on
his poor Duchess, *put away* (I take it so)
        for smiling—at whom?
        Brother Pandolf? or
some visitor to court during the sitting?
        —too generally, if I construe
                        the Duke's clue rightly,
                        to survive the terms
        of his . . . severe protocol. My Lord,
at the time it was delivered to me thus,
        the admonition
        if indeed it was
any such thing, seemed no more of a menace

than the rest of his rodomontade;
              item, he pointed,
            as we toiled downstairs,
      to that bronze *Neptune* by our old Claus
(there must be at least six of them cluttering
    the Summer Palace
    at Innsbruck), claiming
it was "cast in bronze for me." Nonsense, of course.

      But upon reflexion, I suppose
                  we had better take
                  the old reprobate
      at his unspeakable word . . . Why, even
assuming his boasts should be as plausible
    as his avarice,
    no "cause" for dismay:
once ensconced here as the Duchess, your daughter
      need no more apprehend the Duke's
                  murderous temper
                  than his matchless taste.
      For I have devised a means whereby
the dowry so flagrantly pursued by our
    insolvent Duke ("no
    just pretence of mine
be disallowed" indeed!), instead of being
      paid as he pleads in one globose sum,
                  should drip into his
                  coffers by degrees—
      say, one fifth each year—then after five
such years, the dowry itself to be doubled,
    always assuming
    that Her Grace enjoys
her usual smiling health. The years are her

ally in such an arbitrament,
                and with confidence
              My Lord can assure
the new Duchess (assuming her Duke
abides by these stipulations and his own
   propensity for
   accumulating
"semblances") the long devotion (so long as
      he lasts) of her last Duke . . . Or more likely,
          if I guess aright
          your daughter's intent,
   of that young lordling I might make so
bold as to designate her next Duke, as well . . .

             Ever determined in
  My Lordship's service,
  I remain his Envoy
to Ferrara as to the world.
             Nikolaus Mardruz.

Disclaimers

The text of Bach's *St. John Passion*, performed tonight unabridged,
is largely derived from the Gospels, portions of which are alleged
(by some) to be antisemitic. Such passages may well disclose
historical attitudes fastened (by Bach himself) to the Jews,
but must not be taken as having (for that very reason) expressed
convictions or even opinions of the Management or of the cast.

—

The Rape of the Sabine Women, which the artist painted in Rome,
articulates Rubens's treatment of a favorite classical theme.
Proud as we are to display this example of Flemish finesse,
the policy of the Museum is not to be taken amiss:
we oppose all forms of harassment, and just because we have
    shown
this canvas in no way endorses the actions committed therein.

—

Ensconced in the Upper Rotunda alongside a fossil musk-ox,
the giant *Tyrannosaurus* (which the public has nicknamed "Rex"),
though shown in the act of devouring its still-living prey implies
no favor by public officials to zoophagous public displays;
carnivorous Life-Styles are clearly inappropriate to a State
which has already outlawed tobacco and may soon prohibit meat.

Homage to Antonio Canaletto

Venice spent what Venice earned

The operas for which he made designs
in his father's shop
had consequences;
        he never got over the Bibienas'
                                groundless perspectives,
                                and until he died
        such vistas would haunt him: however close
to veritable
palaces he came,
        their porticoes and balustrades composed
                                a proscenium
                                of hysteria.
        But who could count on theaters for pay?
Workmen were always
threatening to quit,
        impresarios "embarrassed," castrati
                                and sopranos in
                                reciprocal fits—
        what could a talent do but "solemnly
excommunicate
the stage" (his own words)
        and set up shop in Rome? A year later
                                he was home again,
                                Roman lessons learned:
        certifiable views of City Life
mattered a good deal
more than the *Scena*
        all'angolo. Unvarying Venice
                                mattered most of all,

           the abiding dream:
   little canals (what else?) colonized by
perfunctory dolls.
First a sketch was made
    (recorded by the *maestro* on the spot),
           then redrawn by him
           more decorously
   indoors, where the *product* could be prepared:
the sky painted in,
sometimes even clouds,
    across the canvas acres, inch by inch,
           and then the contours
           of buildings incised
   into that sky-skin to provide guidance
for eventual
roofs and cornices,
    hemicircles marking an arch, a dome
           (all this done of course
           by apprentices).
At times he was obsessively precise
and in exquisite
detail would devise
    the reigning Doge's coat of arms to fill
           a space smaller than
           a baby's thumbnail
   on the ducal barge; but more likely
San Marco would glow
or gloom as it had
    generations ago. Venice might change,
           storeys be added,
           campaniles fall,
   but master-drawings in the studio
perdured his pattern

Serenissima

　　　years on end, a topographical hoax,

　　　　　　　　　　though one sure to work

　　　　　　　　　　as long as *he* worked:

　　　Grand Tourists continued to pay dear for

proof that they had been

duly discerning

　　　guests of the carnival Republic by

　　　　　　　　　　acquiring views from

　　　　　　　　　　Canaletto's hand.

　　　"His merit lyes in painting things which fall

immediately

under his ogle,"

　　　McSwiny wrote to England. Why not go

　　　　　　　　　　to England as well

　　　　　　　　　　as to Rome? Respite

　　　from the routine of Venetian *vedute*

lured him a moment

that endured ten years:

　　　armed with letters to the Noble Lords, he

　　　　　　　　　　proved (what could he prove?)

　　　　　　　　　　a disappointment

　　　to potential patrons who claimed they saw

deterioration

in his dirty Thames,

　　　and rumors even started he was not

　　　　　　　　　　"the veritable

　　　　　　　　　　virtuoso, no

　　　Canalet at all, but an impostor!"

—easily foiled by

his cool reportage:

　　　a *View of Whitehall* scrupulous enough

　　　　　　　　　　to rout all skeptics.

He stayed on, well-paid
but never (as aristocrats assumed)
to paint their houses,
their horses, their dogs. . . .
Nature he loathed, and next to nature, sport.
Having provided
plausible prospects
of Warwick Castle, Cambridge, Eton, Bath!
he was heard to sigh,
as longed-for Venice
loomed upon his homing horizon, how
glad he was, never
to have to portray
another tree. Another thirteen years'
practice made perfect
sense; he persisted.
Hester Thrale (become Piozzi) bought,
long after his death,
"seven Canalets,
to which his myriad imitators seem
hardly more than a
camera obscura
in the window of a London parlour." . . .
Remembered, required!
in attestation:
"Your own Canalettos will have given
a better idea
of the gondola
than I can convey," a friend of Byron
wrote to Hallam,
and a few years on,
for Théophile Gautier (and not for us?)
Venice had become

"avec ses palais,

    ses gondoles, la ville de Canaletto!"

                    On a last drawing

                    (made inside St. Mark's)

   this busy little man, so early prized

for reproducing

whatever might fall

    under his eye, proudly informs us: "Done

                 without spectacles.

                 A. Canaletto."

Family Values I

After Fuseli: "Milton dictating
Paradise Lost *to his Daughters" 1797*

He was an early riser, four o'clock
mane, even after sight was lost.
He had a man to read to him: the first
language he heard was the Hebrew Bible,
at half-past four. Then he contemplated.
At seven his man came to him again,
reading still, and writing for him, until
dinner, now as much writing as reading.
Of his three daughters, it was Deborah,
the youngest, who could read to him as well,
Italian, French, and Latin, also Greek.
After dinner he would walk some three hours:
he always had a garden where he lived,
and there his exercise was walking till
he went to bed, often-times about nine . . .

ANNE   Deborah will serve, will *also serve,*
bearing his *mild yoke* 'til even she
suffers from what our father likes to call,
when either of us ventures to complain
of lassitude in eye or hand—or mind!—
a bestial and sublunary burning;
then it is my turn. Mary will not come
when we are called, I know not how it is
with her—she manages to stay apart,
and it is always I who must relieve
my sister where she stands, taking the words
from him, terrible words out of the air

as they come, unceasing, to us. I sit,
sewing the while, until our Deborah
fails, and when the silence falls, I begin.

DEBORAH   *Come girls, it is time: I want to be milked!*
such is his humor, so he summons us
—he *would* be cheerful, even in gout-fits—
but no frolic for me, the *faery pen*
he favors over Anne and Mary, far
the better scriveners (nothing he cares
for letters he cannot see, theirs or mine):
Wake to be the word that is your name,
Deborah, bearer of glad tidings, born
through death and known to me by darkness, wake,
utter a song . . . This to my thirteen years.
What does it mean that he will call me his
Cordelia, heart of hearts? Am I the more his
without a mother, and are these sisters
—merely for knowing her—Regan, Goneril?

MARY   There is so much to be hidden, so much
hiding goes along . . . But who calls it such,
a merely surreptitious exploit, when
we know he cannot see what we would hide?
I will not come to this. Let my sisters
wear the red slippers even as they take
down the words of Eve. It shall not be
seen by *my* hand that she rhymes with *deceive.*
Father is cheerful, his sight not so much
lost as retired, "withdrawn into myself,"
he says, "where it sharpens rather than dulls
the edge of my mind." Acuminated thus,
let Anne and Deborah scriven him out,
for I will have no part of *secret things,*

the scandal of the story. I shall wait
and wipe no tears—neither from his blind eyes
nor from my own that see my sisters go
their ways. Deborah looks very like
her father. I am on the distaff side.
What difference can it make or matter?
There is another wife to tend him now,
to wipe the tears forever from his eyes.
I watch them all from my unsuspected
corner in the dark (did I not say there was
hiding done—even father hides something—
though we do not share the things we shroud:
Anne darning her rags, Deborah at the desk,
catching each word upon her cunning quill,
forbidden scarlet on their pretty feet,
and father like some prelate in his chair,
luminous as a gargoyle, and as blind . . .

. . . All the time of writing his Paradise
Lost, *his vein began at the equinox*
each autumn, leaving off at the vernal,
or thereabouts—it was generally May—
pale as the candle that he studied by.
And this for a lustrum at least of his
doing, two years before the king came in,
finishing about three years after
the famous Restoration. Much visited
by the learned, more than he did desire,
and by the gout as well, autumn and spring,
but with this he was blithesome, and would sing.
His widow has his portrait, very like,
which ought to be engraved, the images
before his Works doing him no honor.

Family Values II

After Delacroix: "Milton Dictating
Paradise Lost to his Daughters" 1827

Milton to Leonard Philaras, Athenian (from the Latin):

. . . While yet a little sight remained, when late
I lay in bed and turned to either side,
there used to shine a copious glittering
                    light from my shut eyes.
Then, as my sight grew less from day to day,
such colors as there were decayed; and now,
as if that lucency had grown extinct,
                    it is mere blackness,
or a blackness dashed and woven in
with ashes wont to pour forth of themselves.
Yet such a shadow, still before me now
                    by night as by day,
seems always nearer to a whitish thing,
behaving so that that when the eye should roll,
there is admitted, as through a chink, some
                    charity of light.

    ANNE   It is our Mary picked them, fresh an hour
           ago, and from the garden where you walk
           each evening—where you know the ways. Oh no,
           not here, not now! When is she here with us?
           Mary goes, leaving a summer sweetness,
           and leaves us to *our* ways (you know them too)—
           shall we be on them now? Father, you turn
           aside, indifferent to where I sit
           attending on the words you have prepared.

Giant your hand upon the tablecloth
appears to read its pattern stitch by stitch
thrusting your nails into the Turkey cloth
as if (with blossoms dropping on the wool)
the odor of those roses could be seized
between your thumb and fingers: Touch and Scent
becoming Sight. So what you were you are;
though blind, you see! The spirit afterward,
but first the touch. Your last words, father,
stand just as you spoke them: ". . . *Eternal Spring.*
Not that fair field of Enna . . ." What comes now?

DEBORAH   Ready in arms I hold the lute, knowing
you will have music when the words resist
coming, and coming even, Music Ho!
The poem, you told us, is "like music":
A man must have an ear for it. And some
have none at all. Father, I know you hear
me playing, and when you suddenly speak
the lines our Anne will write, I know you hear
their music too, though music not the same:
I watch you say the lines, holding the lute's
belly against my own, its crooked neck
over my shoulder, and watching I wait
for the silence, for that other music
of yours to cease. Then, father, I begin!
Sometimes, playing, I hear you whisper words
to the strings as they move, and I wonder:
are they already there, such words, or do
my fingers draw them from you with the strings?
Does my music make your music, father?
It is a dim taper, this mind of mine,
and much needs trimming! Which daughter knows,

also serving, what is done best for you:
Anne scrivening? Myself ready with the lute?
Mary, perhaps, who never writes a line,
never plays a note, but leaves beside you
flowers you can only guess, and goes?
O Sound and Scent of Darkness, who is here?

And so, good sir, whatever ray of hope
your famous Greek physicians shed on me,
all the same, as in a case incurable
                    I compose myself,
since as a wise man warns us, many days
of darkness are destined for all, and mine,
amid sweet voices, easier to bear
                    than that deathly one.
What keeps me from resting in the belief
that eyesight lies not in my eyes alone
but, for all purposes of earthly life,
                    in God's providence?
In truth, while only He looks out for me,
leading me forth as with His hand alone,
I shall have given willingly my eyes
                    their long holiday.

Family Values III

After Romney: "Milton and
his Two Daughters" 1794

I leave the garden, as a woman must
leave gardens—*under Father's orders leave*
undeplored cities as well, leave behind
                         whatever places
fathers and husbands, brothers even, say
must be left when there is another life
to be led somewhere, anywhere, *a life*
                    not hers, another's:
that life calls her, therefore she will come in
from the garden, for example, being called
by her father who looks up, *Our Father*
                    who cannot see me
but divines I am here: to me he turns
the crannies that now, with him, pass for eyes,
even as my sisters scribe and sew and
                         give no sign they know
we share the very room: Anne will not look
up from her work, and Deborah looks up
only to watch Father *(watching for me—*
                    what a game we play!
like maypole colors on a broken shaft,
wound over and under: a braid of girls,
and I, the loose ribbon always). All days
                    loose, although not free:
mine the garden tendance, summer days
(Martha not Mary should have been my name)
I keep the briars from the paths he walks,
                         and without a cane

Father *in the cool of the evening* moves
among my roses which the darkness brings
to sweetness, never losing his way. —Look,
                    how the light rises
from Deborah's book, *Father's book as well,*
as if the very verses she takes down
caught fire from her neck and hair, inflaming
                    Annie's profile too
at the touch of that apricot shoulder,
and leaving Father's face a silver mask . . .
I come upon them in the partial dark
                    (I mean, the shadows
serve what is happening, *partial* that way)
and make my outsider's discovery:
this moment has no message, no intent
                    till I descry it!
There has to be a witness to the scene
'to speak of secret things that came to pass
when Beldam Nature in her cradle was,'
                    so Father has said,
or *Bedlam in her crypt,* as I would say . . .
Only because I see my sisters hiding
are they hidden too from the sightless seer
                    who is our father;
only because I enter on this scene
is it a scene composed at all. Just so
God watches us, and makes a meaning
                    for the innocent
as for the guilty. Sisters, which are *we,*
who lead such lives? I like my saying *lead,*
as if our lives, all three, were but some brute
                    within a halter,
to be conducted so. That time I tried

to write for him, as Deborah now writes,
Father's words moved forward *out of silence*
                    and out of darkness
as if to a mark where I sat by him,
so clear I could not write for him again,
despite the times he calls for me to do:
                    '*gathered like a scum*
and settled to itself, such life shall be
in eternal and restless change, self-fed
and self-consumed' . . . Such life, yes: a woman's.
                    There is no garden
untended, no scene unseen. I know that
now, coming in so still and suddenly:
so much for theologics, mine at least!
                    I have read to him
the terrible charges of *ambition,*
contention, corruption, even worse things,
articles of abuse from great doctors,
                    vilifications
of his every word: "pseudo-Quaker!
semi-Arian! Arminian! Mortalist!
Anabaptist! anti-Sabbatarian! Divorcer
                    and polygamist!"
He did not wince, but brushed the words away
like plaguy flies, and only smiled to say,
'*People have a general sense of losing*
                    Paradise but not
an equal gust for the regaining it.'
I wonder what a *Mortalist* can be,
if Father minds so little the misprized
                    acrimination:
how glad he is to begin each day's task
with the other girls, mortal certainly

as he himself, though cherished beyond life:
                    'the different sex,
in most resembling unlikeness, and most
unlike resemblance, cannot but please best
in aptitude of that variety
                    and be pleased as well . . .'
Soon it will be time for his evening walk.
Leaving the girls to wonder, Father will
come to the door where he must know I am,
                    as he knows the time
for walking. He will touch me on his way
and murmur *duty's done.* My raked gravel
yields to his certain steps. The path is clear.
                    Father, duty's done.

Family Values IV

After Mihàly Munkàcsy:
"Milton Dictating Paradise Lost
to his Daughters" 1877
Collection: New York Public Library
(in restoration, not on exhibit
at the present time)

17 March, 1877

"So there it is. And there we are. Good Lord,
     was it worth all the nuisance
of coaxing mother's seamstress to run up
     those awful gowns? Enduring
Klàra's constant recital—*in English!*—
     of that impossible poem
which I can't follow even in French? (Why
     honor it as eternal
merely because it seems to be endless?)
     Hours of posing to become
the dreariest of the daughters, sewing
     away in shade and shadow,
after Rembrandt's manner, as father says . . ."

"But Ilona, at least you're looking at
     father—I mean, *their* father:
Milton brooding as if he were not blind,
     not yet gray either, wearing
trousers with silver buckles at each knee:
     more Cromwellian, I'd say,
than Miltonic, whatever that may be . . .
     Look at *me,* standing there like
some petulant housemaid (those hands!), staring
     into the dark—or the light,

does it matter which?—turning her back
    in a fit of the sulks on
the virginals she refuses to play . . ."

"Don't be so vain about it! The point is
    that all three faces are quite
destitute of daughterly affection
    or admiration—Mary
(that's you, Julia) shallow and sullen,
    Anne self-willed and passionless,
though how Munkàcsy could make Ilona
    into a Mozart *soubrette*! . . .
And as for me, scribe Deborah, watching
    our father's lips for language
beyond my comprehension: who *is* that
    tired blue-stocking but one more
termagant, bored as the two of you?"

"There's no argument then: we'll make father
    give the grim machine away—
why keep a record of the Szechenys
    we know will betray us all
the moment our backs are turned—the moment,
    my dear sisters, we are dead?
Klàra, *you're* his favorite, *you* tell him
    all that money spent on famous
Maestro Munkàcsy is wasted . . ."
                              "Not if he
    can unload it onto some rich
Yankee as dim about Count Szecheny

as about our own dear identities—
    he'll care if it's Ilona
who sings, Julia who plays, Klàra who writes
    about as much as he'd care

which nameless spectre . . ."
                    "I've *told* you their names:
    Mary, Deborah, and Anne,
the poet Milton's daughters whom we are
    honored to incarnate."
                    "Let
the wretched thing go—we have our photographs;
    we have our own father too,
and after all, we are Hungarians!"

17 March, 1977

    To the Director, Administrative
    Officers, Executives and Trustees
    of the Astor (now Public) Library,
                of New York City.
    Dear Sirs, I address you in confidence,
    although the League by which I am empowered
    (I hold the mission as a sacred trust)
    to preserve, defend, indeed to pursue
                National Honor,
    has authorized me, should our petition
    be disallowed, to seek Public Support;
    nor shall I shrink from disclosing the more
    flagitious vicissitudes of the case
                to those newspapers
    likely, in their liberal stance, to share
    our view of the matter which inspires
    the proposal below. It is my hope,
    however, that no such recourse will be
                necessitated,
    and that a private appeal to your sense
    of Justice and Decorum will suffice . . .

"It will not do, dear Arpàd, to begin
on a minatory note, if you mean
to tumble down to grumbling once
you make your point. Besides, you leave us with
a distinct impression (if I understand
correctly what 'flagitious' means—must you
mount quite so high a horse, merely because
you want something?) that our own family
is to blame . . . We have done nothing wrong, dear,
and Aunt Ilona would be horrified
by even a hint of hanky-panky
connected with the Szechenys. What case*?"*

Let me begin, then, by reminding you
that precisely a century ago
          Astor's own nephew,
prompted by that public-minded zeal
marking the American Maecenas,
bestowed as a gift quite in the spirit of
the institution he offered it to
          a work of high art,
"The Poet Milton Dictating *Paradise*
Lost to his Daughters" by M. Munkàcsy,
our painter with perhaps the surest claim
on our sentiments as on our savants
          to be considered
modern Hungary's national artist.
Granted a Gold Medal at the Paris
Salon that year, his picture was admired
in New York by twelve thousand visitors
          the first two months
of its presentation in the Great Hall
where, until recently, it has remained . . .

"Arpàd, where are you? Tell them what you want
and be done with it. Enough of your breathing
about the bush—come out of the shrubbery!"

Dear Sirs, a century's neglect—unconscious,
I have no doubt—has taken its toll, and
    bitumen has dimmed
the once jewel-like colors; moreover
the load of so many meters of paint
has dragged the canvas almost off its frame—
the whole contraption, high above the stairs,
    droops alarmingly . . .
And such dilapidation is for us
a timely sign the work should be returned
to the country of its creator. Here
we shall undertake to restore it all
    to its initial
circumstance, its pristine predicament,
so to speak. For such a task, we possess
the artist's *modello* in Budapesth—
very clear as to values, the color
    of light in shadow—
and once in our hands, the work will be made
indistinguishable from what it was
originally . . .

  "Really, Arpàd, you must avoid that tone:
  you are not blaming *anyone, you are*
  calling attention to a patriot's
  duty. Here is your opportunity
  to sound—to strike!—the family-toga note . . ."

        . . . Political events
of the last few decades make any such
transfer of ownership only the more
                telling, and the grand
Miltonic themes of Freedom and Conscience
assume their proper national stature
at this time. You may regard this letter,
gentlemen, as a *modello* itself,
                preliminary
to those formal transactions which of course
must follow the satisfaction granted
by your concurrence with the undersigned
(a lineal scion of Count Szecheny
                who commissioned our
"Milton Dictating *Paradise Lost* . . . ," and
grandson of that same Klàra Szecheny
who "sat" for Mihàly Munkàcsy's so
deteriorated . . .

        "Arpàd!"
                . . . masterpiece),
        Yours,
                Arpàd Mayr.

Memo, May 1977
Solicitation rejected, and filed
with other crackpot correspondence re
art-works listed among the Library's
                permanent holdings.

Family Values V

November 15

    Dear Professor Nicolson, Would you be
so good as to stop by my Gallery
at your convenience to help us with
the presentation of a new canvas
                  by René Magritte?
'Family Values,'
Magritte has informed us, is his tribute
to Fuseli's masterpiece (now on view
at the Art Institute of Chicago):
'Milton Dictating *Paradise Lost*
              to his Three Daughters').

Not surprisingly
for works by either artist, there have been
iconographic questions and even
charges (in Belgium) of obscenity!
Your Columbia colleague Professor
                Meyer Schapiro
suggests that a word
from a noted Miltonist like yourself
would go far—farther than the evasive
assessments of any mere art critic—
toward reconciling Mrs. Grundy with
                the revelations,
startling as they are,
of Magritte's vision. Furthermore, I am
myself convinced, Professor Nicolson,
that granted the prestige of your immense
authority, Magritte's new creation
                might work its magic
unobstructed by the philistinism

which has so often blighted the careers
of Ernst and Balthus, Belmer and the rest.
We look forward to meeting you. Warmly,
                              Julien Levy

November 19

                              Mr. Levy, please.
Marjorie Nicolson. Yes. And you are
Julien Levy himself? I had supposed
                    there would be a staff:
your letter mentioned "we" several times.
Delighted to meet you too. Now where . . . Oh,
                    please don't call me that:
'professor' just makes static in my ears
and puts off any kind of intercourse
                    with actual learning.
I much prefer that you would think of me
as Chairman of the English Department.
                    No, *Chairman* will do.
The gender affixed to "chair" hardly seems
a matter of controversy; perhaps
                    you have guessed as much
from the fashion (or non-fashion?) in which
I dress. It has been said, Mr. Levy,
                    though not to my face,
that I look like a tweed fireplug with breasts.
Absurd simile: fireplugs, as you know,
                    already have breasts! . . .
In any case, as the Department Chair
—surely I look more like a chair to you,
                    even a sofa,
than a fireplug, don't I, Mr. Levy?—
and as the author of five studies (six
                    counting the Handbook)

in explication of Miltonic *facts*,
I eschew the padding of *Professor*—
                    quite superfluous.
"Miss Nicky" is what my friends and students
—I hope they are the same?—often call me.
                    Perhaps you will too . . .
The one problem I met with, arriving
in my character as a full-bodied
                    piece of furniture,
is the design of the elevators
in these old houses: making others wait,
                    a solo ascent
was my only means of approach. But here
I am . . . and there, I guess, is your Magritte!
                    I've done my homework,
and I'm proud to be consulted: rarely
is an academic figure—*e.g.*, mine!—
                    asked to mediate
among sin, sales, and Surrealism . . .
I am assuming that Magritte is still,
                    if not in favor
with Monsieur Breton, a Surrealist?
These Movements are momentary as
                    the Protestant sects
were for poor Milton . . . And this canvas here,
this grand machine, this Conversation Piece
                    has been called obscene?
And immoral too! Well of course it is
a complex issue—Shakespeare was hardly
                    the first to present
a father whose feelings for three daughters
infringe on our notions of seemliness.
                    From the very start,
Apollo and the Muses afforded

another instance of such intimate

                promiscuities . . .
I am not familiar with Fuseli's
picture to which Magritte pays homage,

                yet I cannot see
how any knowledge of it could keep me
from asserting the inoffensiveness

                of this brilliant work.
Of course it is difficult to explain
why the daughters should *all* have fish-heads

                and yet be wearing
no clothes at all . . . But obscene? immoral?
The way the poet—don't you agree

                that must be Milton
up there?—is lying almost on top of
the three . . . girls leads me to suppose

                Magritte is punning
on "milt"—fish sperm, you know—*milt on*:
an incestuous poetry with his

                ichthycephalous
daughters . . . Oh dear, I suppose that does sound
rather obscene, though it's a classical

                trope for Apollo.
The longer I look, the less I know what
to think. Magritte's title is certainly,

                like many of his,
odd and perhaps perverse. I'm thinking of
The Invisible World and *Siren Song*—

                Family Values,
when you add that jointed sarcophagus
to all the fishy goings-on . . . I fear

                such figurations
may indeed offend an orthodox sense
of propriety—Milton often does!

                To stand fast against

such defensive folly, best to recall
what Milton himself, hard-pressed by righteous
                              objectors, remarked:
They thought themselves gallants, and I thought them
fools; they made sport, and I laughed; they misspoke
                              and I misliked; and,
to make up the atticism, they were out
and I hissed . . . I must thank you once again
                              for my Private View,
which I trust will soon become a public
occasion. Please don't try to see me out:
                              the elevator,
as I told you, necessitates my making
an altogether solo departure.
                              Of course if any
attestation from the resident
Miltonist of Columbia can be
                              of some assistance,
I shall be delighted to oblige. Thanks,
again, for this experience. Good bye,
                              Mr. Levy. Down!

THE JULIEN LEVY GALLERY
132 East 57 Street NYC

requests the honor
of your presence at the opening
of an exhibition of works by René Magritte
December 12 from 5 to 7
featuring *Family Values*, a new painting

"No modern canvas has
given me more pleasure."
—*Professor Marjorie Nicolson*

Mrs. Eden in Town for the Day

Sorry I'm late. I had to drive *way* out of my
    way to pick up coyote piss—
for the garden. We use about a quart a month:
    it really does deter the deer.

This man I know at the zoo keeps it for me, for
    a group of us, actually:
all gardeners. He happens to *be* a keeper—
    of coyotes, hyenas, wolves,

whatever—and he keeps coyote piss as well
    (under refrigeration, of course),
sells it right there at the zoo. I hate the long drive,
    but I love having no more deer

in the garden. Expensive, too, or should I say
    dear, but it's definitely not
a competitive item—where else can you get
    coyote piss that's full strength,

not reconstituted from crystals or some kind
    of concentrate? It has to be
fresh—from the wild—or the damn deer just ignore it.
    I wonder how such merchandise

would be collected? Tom says there's something
    they call a Texas Catheter,
really not much more than a perforated
    condom attached to a bottle . . .

Have you ever seen such goings-on at a *zoo?*
    Well neither have I—but of course
I wasn't looking . . . Who would be, unless you *knew* . . .
    However he gets hold of it,

it works! Today our keeper told me *human hair*
    has the same effect, on most deer—
we could try that. Think how much cheaper, for one thing:
    a year's sweepings from Tom's barber

would cost less than a week's gasoline! Even so,
    people's hair . . . Better the other:
I wonder which animals would keep off if we tried
    our own instead of coyotes'?

moose   dikdik   gazelle   caribou   hartebeest   gnu

The Job Interview

with André Breton, 1957

The question, Monsieur Gracq advised, had best
be asked, and answered, in the Old Lion's den:
would I, duly scrutinized, be allowed
              to translate *Nadja?*

Factors in my favor: I did speak French
—the one parlance necessarily shared—
and my links to certain Proscribed Figures
              were, to him, unknown.

Bravely enough, therefore, I proceeded
through the Place Blanche and up the Rue Fontaine,
though in my heart (or in some other place)
              I knew the danger:

Breton's legendary loathing of queers . . .
Ever since Jacques Vaché had overdosed
on opium in a Nantes hotel, naked
              with another man,

Surrealism's pope had unchurched men
of my kind, condemned our "perverted race"
to a paltry outer darkness, claiming
              he could sense, could *smell*

an intolerable presence . . . Fee fo fum.
Climbing his stairs, I wondered if I gave
off the emanations of turpitude:
              would he detect me

by the scent of my "disgusting practice"?
Was I entitled to conceal from him
—indeed *could* I conceal the taint which made
           whatever talent

I might have merely an interference,
an imposture? A scuffle of slippers,
and the author of *Nadja* let me in
           past the museum

of surreal objects, himself another
museum of sorts, who had shown epigones
how to read, how to live, and how to love.
           Some epigones.

Others had failed—rejections, suicides;
of which no hint discolored our encounter,
affable to a fault. Perhaps the three
           decades since Nadja

had revealed to the world her Accidents
of Sublimity had blunted Breton's
erotic stipulations: and I was so
           pusillanimous

as to keep my *tendencies* to myself,
where they fluttered helplessly enough:
of course I knew in my heart that the one
           surrealist act

—O coward heart! would be to challenge this
champion of liberation, this foe of all
society's constraints, but I could do
           nothing of the kind,

nor need I have. O reason not the need:
I left the Master of the Same New Things
with every warrant of his trust in me
                    as his translator

(*Traditorre—tradutore!* in fact,
if not in French), and forty years have passed
since that traduced encounter. Where are we?
                    Nadja in English

is still in print, and people still hate queers.
I allay that heart of mine with the words
Breton wrote to Simone, first of his wives
                    (and a Jew like me):

criticism will be love, or will not be.

For Mona Van Duyn, Going On

As for me, I lost
all sense of human possibility

Blacking out, we say; but it was more like
ablution in the Country of the Blue,
that region of "altogether elsewhere,"
   possibly sacred . . .
Arriving hungry after airborne hours
for a Poetry Festival, I had
fainted among my fellow bards, offstage.
   Out of the blue, then,
came (before I could recognize your face)
your voice, incredulous squeal that oddly
mixed with carpet-figures and the fragrance
   of Spray-O-Vac Rose:

"Richard, *you* passed out!" The accusation
was evident: any *évanouissement*
to be sanctioned here was really your thing,
   and my spill or spell
on the floor—though I had no notion of
its drama at the time: leave that to you!—
was probably a version of that same
   "drive for attention"
to which, mother said, I was always prone
(surely the *mot juste* now). In any case,
I knew I had no such viable contacts
   with the Other Side,

no likely means of recuperating
messages left indecipherable
unless I put myself to Mona's School:
   where else grapple with

such hard-won experience, no sooner gained
than gainsaid by means of your so-envied
rhetorical conversion-hysteria.
    Such was the lesson
of your lyceum—no wonder you laid claim
or likely connoisseurship at the least
to these episodes of "fallings from us" . . .
    In a life given

to any of these obliterations,
to debility, danger and despair,
let it come down! as the Second Murderer
    famously remarks;
make no attempt to spare anyone grief,
but Go For It, fail without fail, settle
down at the center of the worst and wait
    there for whatever
news we never hoped or hated to hear
half so much, despatches you especially
listened for and lovingly retrieved: not
    to know anything,

but only to be looking for something,
renouncing the possession of wisdom
in favor of the power to observe.
    Most of us, Mona,
spoil our poems (our lives) because we have
ideas—not ideas but approved topics
that can be carried around intact. Oh
    watch me faint once more,
and this time make a true recovery:
acceptance of the vast erroneous
community of pain to which we all
    belong. No ideas

but in nothing! No failures but those proved!
To become poets, *to become* human,
never *to be,* for as soon as we "are"

   we are no longer
human perhaps, nor even poets . . . Once
I had come to, I obeyed Van Duyn's Law:
we only are by virtue of (it *is*

   a virtue, I guess)
our continual tendency not to be . . .
You scraped me off the floor, and we performed
our poems in a state of perfect health—

   until the next time.

Lee Krasner: *Porcelain*, a Collage

oil and paper on panel,
30 × 48 inches, 1955

Take it down Tear it up Turn it over Make
    it new out of old makings:
exert what that venerable scatterbrain
    in Weimar once called the Power
of Pulling Yourself Together whereby
    the master is first revealed.
Exposed is more like it: shown for what you are.

Porcelain! If a watched pot never boils, what
    happens to a pulverized one?
These are not heroic fragments, nothing here
    inherently shapely! No
identifiable vessel remains: you
    picked up the pieces all
over the place and laid them down again

according to your own ragged politics
    of reaching and retracting, no
better than breathing really, putting mere drips,
    untimely ripp'd, not so much
where you saw they belonged, but how you surrendered
    to their various discomfort:
an open mind must be open at both ends!

The wrong papers, the wretched old canvases
    discovered to be no more
than rehearsals for much new catastrophe:
    this purple patch, that sliver
of viridian woven into the web
    of accommodating earth,
our only planet not named for some god . . .

Then glued these scraps, these scrapings, these scrupulous
        approximations to some
consistent field of accidents all that year, once
        your wild partner in chrom-
atic fantasy had spilled himself out of
        life like a puddle of paint:
these exist only because they have been made to—

compelled, this time, to sort together without
        alienation, which means
they are a final vision. No, semi-final,
        since the whole soul is never
one, save in ecstasy and not merely when,
        as Yeats declared, it has been
rent. Another twenty years had to be lived

before there were Krasner collages again,
        entire paintings ripped to shreds
to let the white light through. But that was when
        you were dying, as you knew.
Meanwhile, there were other allowances
        to be made, other makings
allowed. You decided once again to paint.

A Sibyl of 1979

The river lay white that afternoon, the highway too—
    apparently frozen to a standstill.
Muriel Rukeyser hobbled to her high window,
    standing beside me, both of us looking
down at the big meat-trucks parked on West Street, empty now
    but not as they would be after dark, men
furtively climbing in and out, walking away fast.

"Do you ever go to the trucks, Richard—go inside?"
    her voice close to my ear, low, determined.
The question, its very tone, took me by surprise: so
    she knew what that meant, *going to the trucks*—
even in the dead of winter, the cherished, feckless
    secret of many who still persisted . . .
And even if she did know, the question surprising:

were we on those terms? What terms? "Dangerous, isn't it—"
    the voice persistent as she took my arm
"doing . . . what you do, inside there?" Staring down at them,
    I told her I never went to the trucks.
"I'm glad. That's not a judgment, only relief. Only
    my own cowardice, really . . . Dear Richard,
I asked you here because I want to give you something

you may be able to use. I can't. When they sent me
    home from the hospital, after my stroke,
it was right here, this computer-thing: supposed to be
    helpful because it changes what you write
so easily, so easily restores what you change . . .
    I tried it a while, but it doesn't work
for me: I don't need to change things so much any more,

not the way you do, my cautious friend. I'm past changing."
    About the trucks nothing more was said, and
I took the virtually virgin computer home
    and plugged it in. Nothing occurred, until
a few days later, my fingers "wandering idly"
    (just as in Sir Arthur's *Lost Chord*!) over
the unresponsive keys, these sentences appeared, words

she had abandoned, "past changing" now: *No thought wakens*
    without waking others . . . There is one proof
of ability, only one: doing it! . . . The more
    you love yourself, the more you are your own
worst enemy . . . Seers don't need to be observers . . . We keep
    learning—involuntarily, even—
and finally we learn to die. Muriel learned, and died,

but reading her words the screen retained—sortilege? poems?
    I faltered: time was, if you lost even
a tenth part of the Sibyl's leaves, you too would be lost . . .
    Was now the time when if you kept even
a tenth part you were saved, as a frightened man is saved
    by words? *You will not be deprived because*
your dreams did not come true, but because you never dreamed.

The Sibyl, Petronius reports, could not die, only
    wither away until she was so small
she survived in a leather bottle, pleading for death.
    Muriel's bottle was her own body;
I bring her words up on that pale, superseded screen
    where they glow like omens, benefactions:
Everything you really possess was given to you.

—

A post-script, seventeen years afterwards. The gift
   I bring would be quite as bewildering
to you as that computer: what would you make, Muriel,
   of a CD claiming to reproduce
(on the right contraption) *The Song of the Sibyl*—words
   the very ones Aeneas might have heard,
music from as late as the Tenth Century? . . . My offering.

The Twain Meeting

for Anne Hollander

Tokyo, 1992

A priest leads us into the inner court
(Supplementary Offering required—
otherwise you clap and bow with the rest

who toss their coins into a grate outside
the paling: unprofessional prayer)
of the pine-muffled Meiji Jingu Shrine,

like most things in Japan a replica,
this one paid for by the pauperized
citizens after "our" raids of '45;

the original opened as late as
1920, though the cypress *torii*
—largest in the country—are made of wood

easily (or hardly: what do I know?)
over a thousand years old. Here in one
of the city's twenty-three hearts

looms a forest convened from each Province,
where newlyweds (in kimono, for once!)
wander sadly; and on the Grand Last Day,

Omisoka, a crowd of two million
arrives to hear the New Year tolled in by
108 peals of a bell. Enough numbers!

Once we are inside the roofless precinct,
and once our prayer is selected (World Peace,
we are advised), the priest and his helper

in white linen frocks esoterically
tucked and tied, set off by patent-leather
pattens and a matching black crest, decide

propitious moment to bang the drum
hanging over all our heads. Now! and Now!
whereupon the prayer is read (by us!),

sake and ceremonial candy bestowed,
we sign the ledger and are quickly shown
out. Ears still ringing from that demon drum,

we glance back: at his desk, the priest picks up
a cordless phone and (our guide Kondo reports)
starts an argument with his new boyfriend.

Exhibition

New and enormous, Tokyo City Hall
is based, or spired, for all its ninety floors,
on the Basilica of Chartres, flaunting
two gray-granite *flèches*. Safer in earthquakes
than all the paper acres they replace,
"the towers sway—like bamboo," Miss Ito smiled,

as she squired us from the Governor's suite
to an even higher eyrie. Here they were:
sixty years of droll *New Yorker* covers
displayed to appreciative giggles from
officials' wives in kimono (this, too,
a rite, like moon-viewing: on with the old!)

whose slow queue round the gallery we joined,
horrified to discover (the one right word),
as each bright oblong snapped into recall,

how many renditions of our urban
anthropology were derisive japes,
clever taunts, Orientalist lampoons!

Of course for six of those years "they" had been
The Enemey; of course "we" vilified
every apparent sign of otherness—
teeth, eyes, eyeglasses, hair, height, gait, and girth—
employing, long after hostilities,
all the resources of racial disdain

to put down or hold up to ridicule
anything not ourselves, our scene, our sense
of unanswerable Manhattan Style—
didn't we have some towers of our own?
Yet the choice of these humiliations
had been "theirs": Miss Ito herself had hung

these all-too-prepossessing emblems, *proud*
of the honorable responsibility . . .
Grinning dreadfully in the Express Car,
we dropped like a bomb down eighty-some floors
to the intractable city below,
wondering who had been humbled: *Banzai!*

The Intimate Art of the Little Paper Costume
Bridegroom Shop, Takashimaya

Read the instructions first. Then
all you need is a sharp pair of scissors,
    nimble fingers, and spare time.
Tape, after frequent and vigorous use,
    may provide reinforcement,
but glue is not required in most cases:
    once the paper is folded,
a system of tabs and slits will suffice.

Remember, check your own size
against those on the diagram enclosed
    to guarantee a firm but
comfortable fit. Cut only those slits
    consistent with your measurements
so as not to weaken the paper with
    too many holes. An artist's
sketch on the page facing the diagram

    will give some indication
how to keep the costume of your choice
    from falling off (such accidents
are likely to distract you and even
    inhibit the natural
flow of action and dialogue; after all,
    you want the series of Calls
and Replies to be uninterrupted) . . .

    In time and with practice,
a whole new dimension can be added
    to your own (and your partner's)
experience of pleasure. Initially,
    though, you would be well-advised
to choose a single design suitable
    to your personality:
The Rose, perhaps, or The Locomotive—

    later on you may want to
experiment with some of the bolder
    costumes: The Dragon, say,
or The Moth, even The Space Shuttle!
    Whatever your choice, the main
purpose of the Little Paper Costume
    will be served: to put you
in touch with the self of your wilder dreams.

Some clients may feel at ease
experimenting from the very start
    with the entire range of these
Costumes, but we suggest that most users
    will benefit from limited
and gradual wear. Especially in
    first encounters, we advise
a blend of recognition and surprise.

Whatever your choice, the main
purpose of the Little Paper Costume
    will be served: to discover
your innermost expressive fantasies,
    indeed, to realize them
by utilizing the traditional
    imaginative methods
and principles of Japanese design.

Anxieties

The sound of the *kanji* character for death
is the same as the sound of the one for 4
(as in "for 4"), so place-settings always come
in fives, and "you will notice in hospitals
            there is no fourth floor."

What made Mr. Sato continually
interrupt with such questions? Why did Kenji
            answer so vaguely?

Responsive interjections, *aizuchi*,
play a crucial part in communicating
with Japanese people, who feel uneasy
if the person listening to them speak
            should remain silent.

Why did Mrs. Kawakami tell David
her husband was ill? What could have made Yoko
act the way she did?

The Japanese themselves have difficulty
remembering each other's names; at all times
they carry cards (*meishi*) which they will exchange
even when it is extremely unlikely
   they will meet again.

Why was Makoto so embarrassed? What did
Anne do to cause Professor Toda's response?
   Was the waiter rude?

Though you may wish to make a note, do not write
directly on another person's *meishi*
in his presence or put it in your back-pocket
wallet: when you sit down, you will be *sitting*
   on the *meishi.*

Why did Mr. Yamashita assume
he and his wife must have stayed too long?
   Was Kazuo disturbed?

Use both hands to receive presents in Japan:
it is a culture which makes no distinction
between left and right, though many Japanese
will be dismayed when American guests eat
   noodles noiselessly.

Why did Miss Ito's husband look so puzzled
the first time Richard said, or attempted to
   say, konnichiwa?

The Japanese people do not have as much
intentional body contact as we do:
touching in a crowded train is meaningless,
impersonal, and unavoidable besides.

But hugging is out . . .

*What should Michiko do at this point? Why did
Yasuko walk away? Was Mrs. Uemura
flustered or amused?*

Further Triangulations

after an initial three, some years back

I've almost finished papering the whole
of what you, in your florid way, would call
the foyer and the little downstairs john

with all your recent letters (yellowing fast).
That way I'll keep the record straight without
—quite—having to get rid of them *or* you:

In almost every case they're wrong side up,
and even when, to fit them round the pipes
behind the toilet, they've been pasted so

the words could be made out, you can be sure,
with handwriting as prodigal as yours
(florid, let's say), the risk of prying eyes

is pretty low . . . And who would pry but you
and me? Besides, according to the old
Florentine master, *time will darken it.*

Talk, my dear, about darkening! ever since
Elizabeth died, there's been a general
loss of light—haven't you noticed it?

She lived with you (if you want to call that living),
she lived with me (whether you want to or not):
from which I deduce, a woman must have the strength

to choose what she prefers and cling to it:
otherwise, better die. And Elizabeth died.
I think you left her because she could not give

precisely what she was able to give to me:
the gratifications of vanity. That must be why
I was so faithful. And you never were,

unless you count your episodes with me
as a kind of faith to her. Do you? Can you?
It certainly takes some calculating, our

entanglements, and that's what I intend
doing a while, unless I am cut off
in the flower of my middle age. I must have said

all this to you, but hear it once again:
the past is past because it forms a part
of our present, of what we are by *having been*;

because, in short, it is OUR past. I guess
that means you'd better come. Don't write again,
letters are no use now, just come. I'll wait.

So often the best solution, or the only one,
is to abandon the problem. The way she has
abandoned us. She left me . . . quite well-fixed,

as I guess you know. *Fixed* is the operative
word. By coming, you can release us both
(and probably unstick your letters too).

The Manatee

New Smyrna Beach, Florida

She never took much credit for "The Moose"
   —"it all just happened that way"—
and sent our questions packing as abuse

of her privacy; Elizabeth Bishop would say
   enough had been said, would smile,
and class, we knew, was over for the day.

We longed to ask her, "Why, why do we feel
   this sweet sensation of joy?"
an ecstasy attributed to all

of us on that bus of hers . . . Was that the only
   appropriate response when
some great big (harmless) lummox "happened" by?

Had it been joy for Robert Frost (a man
   more likely to feel alarm
than unaccountable delight upon

being looked over by an Alien Form)
   that time Whatever-it-was
appeared to him "as a great buck" and swam

providentially out of sight across
   the pond? Would either poet
make common cause with odd affects like those

of Witold Gombrowicz (who, I admit,
   is an apocalyptic
sort of witness)? In June, 1958,

G was walking down a eucalyptus-
      lined avenue when a cow
sauntered out from behind a tree. "I stopped,

and we looked each other in the eyes; so
      tense was the moment I lost
my bearings *as a man*—that is, you know,

as a member of our race. It was the first
      time, apparently, I was
experiencing the shame of a Man come face

to face with an Animal. What then ensues
      is obvious: one becomes
an Animal also, and uneasy, as

if Nature, on all sides, were watching." Shame!
      Fear! Joy!—reactions vary
strongly when we meet The Other, it seems,

but given such discrepant histories,
      I realized that our great
human hope, watching the manatee rise

or emanate—no other verb could state
      so well the means of its ap-
parition: a *manatee* must *emanate*—

out of its New Age of jeopardized sleep
      in the slime of Turnbull Bay,
is to greet The Other (whatever gap

grins between us) as Another—let's say,
      members of a cast one is
proud to share the Comedy with today.

Les Travaux d'Alexandre

bronze, 23 inches, 1967

for Dominique de Menil

My dear Magritte, I'm glad to be in touch
again and, in the nature of the thing,
quite literally, bumping into one
of your last works, eighth in the disputed
succession of those "sculptures" you had seen
only in wax, never the finished bronze—
though you did make a finicky design
for this heroic object (one of five
to which as ever an unlikely name
seems to have been fastened from the start).

By all accounts such naming was a group
affair: you and your cronies and Georgette
would think up proper titles, so to speak,
once creation was put paid, a done thing,
hence ever to be known by that device . . .
When all his conquering was over and
Asia in his grasp, the hero wept:
his past deleted by his present put
his future beyond him. You called this work
Alexander's Labors, of course! What else?

Moreover, dear master, colliding with
this culminal object, I summon up
the apposite sense of what's past, passing,
or coming to pass (as your fancy name
for it, for once, makes ultimately plain):

held fast within the octopine embrace
of a burly root, confined there surely
since sapling days, a most efficient axe
is clearly captive of the very tree
it has, just now, reduced to a mere stump.

Your paradox so inverately
enacted—back to front or night by day,
every antithesis which brings about
the extermination of time—what's that
but the task of any art? You made it
more sudden, more seditious maybe, but
is it not the same, this quattrocento
panel by Benozzo Gozzoli, say,
his *Dance of Salome*, where on the right,
gown eddying from her completed turn,

the girl demands what, in a sinister
niche, the glamorous executioner
prepares to . . . execute, though far upstage
Salome (again! the same gold folds, but
docile here) presents her scarlet mother with
the head she still must ask for on the right.
"The same," but more fiercely epitomized
in your harsh emblem. Maybe that's the cost
of our modernity: the death of time
instanter! and we have misread the signs—

what if *this* is time's real life: the salvered
head in her mother's lap which Salome
implores unsevered from the living saint . . .
What if *only* a rootbound axe can fell
the tree that has overgrown it in time—

not in our silly sequence, our *and then* . . .
but in that Other Time, my dear Magritte,
the time you told by one wonder after
the next, till the hero's labors were done
and wonders had to cease. Wherefore these tears.

My Last Hustler

. . . all smiles stopped

When "Brad" is lying naked, or rather naked is lying
in wait for whatever those he refers to as clients require
by way of what *they* refer to as satisfaction, denying
himself the distraction of alcohol or amyl, there appears
in his eyes no flicker of shame, no flare of shameless desire,
and what tribute he is paid finds him neither tender nor fierce.

On a bed above suspicion, creases in obviously fresh
linen still mapping a surface only a little creamier than
the creaseless hills and hollows of his compliant flesh,
Brad will extend himself (as the graphic saying goes)
and the upper hand—always his—will push into place *the man
who happens to be there* till happening comes to blows

(another saying you now more fully grasp): full-blown,
Brad will prepare himself, though not precipitately,
for the grateful-kisses stage; he offers cheek and chin
but objects to undergoing your accolade on his mouth:
he has endured such homage too early, too often, too lately,
and for all his boyish ways Brad is not wholly a youth.

Routines on some arduous rigging, however, can restore
him to himself in mirrors, every which way surrounded
by no more than what he seems and mercifully *by no more.*
Booked by a merciless Service for a thousand afternoons,
Brad will become the needs of his "regulars" confounded
by his indifferent regard, by his regardless expense . . .

Take him—young faithful!—there and then. Marvel! praise!
Fond though your touch may be and truly feeling your tact,

yet a mocking echo returns—remote, vague, blasé—
of Every Future Caress, so very like your own!
However entranced the scene you make (the two of you act
as one to all appearance, but one is always alone),

derision will come to mind, or to matter over mind:
the folly, in carnal collusion, of mere presented *skill*.
Undone, played out, discharged, one insight you will have gained
which cannot for all these ardent lapses be gainsaid
—even his murmured subsidence an exercise of will—
is the sudden absolute knowledge Brad would rather be dead.

Avarice, 1849: A Distraction

My dear Balzac, you must remain quite still.
    Make no motion at all, or nothing
will appear on the plate but a faint grisaille,

    the Unknown Masterpiece indeed!
Though mine is a drastically lesser gift,
    let me attempt to entertain you

or at least to keep your spirit occupied
    while the flesh is forcibly idle.
Between exposures (that is our rakish name

    for the interval when light's pencil
is permitted to limn your face) you may speak,
    but you must not shift your attitude;

I have found that unobtrusive clamp behind
    the nape to be of great assistance—
don't you agree? Then let us begin. Of course

    I have hoped for such an occasion
in order to speculate with you . . . Oh no,
    nothing like an interrogation,

merely these musings intended to beguile
    an intellect that has awed all France.
Ready now? No moving until I signal . . .

It has been, sir, a constant bewilderment
    since I first came to the *Comedy*
—reading for over a decade now—that you,

    having anatomized Greed as well
as Molière, abstain from all condemnation;
    and that an author who engenders

such unflagging monsters of avarice as
a Grandet, a Gobseck, a Goriot!
nonetheless hits off his dismaying portraits

of all that is worst in humankind
without a single condemnation of sin—
as if the creator draws no line

between Avarice and Wanting? Book after
book declares all human happiness
comes down to numbers, figures, sums—as if

counting were the same thing as loving!
No, no, don't speak yet! Not till the plate records
a face that contradicts all logic:

the parts so much greater than the whole . . . Indulge
my lens but one more moment, then
you may correct my views as wisdom sees fit:

if Not To Have is the onset of Desire,
then isn't actual having—such *owning*
as you so exhaustively articulate—

isn't possessing in that kind . . . culpable?
Now you may speak, but please to retain
the same pose, we must attempt at least one more. . . .

Nadar, dear fellow, you do not read me well.
In literature, who can believe
he has ever been understood? We all die

alone. See here: when you speak the word
avarice, *when you utter the verb* to have,
feel how fondly your front teeth caress

your lower lip: that is how the meaning comes,
*   our bodies making out, making up*
the sense of words. . . . Our senses make it: avid!

*   my friend, as eager to own the self*
as the mouth to own the tongue. Read me better:
*   I see no sin in loving what we own,*

for indeed we own nothing save what owns us—
*   our tongues, for instance—we own nothing!*
The one sin is to believe, indeed behave

*   as if we own what we love: I wrote*
as much a million times, I shall keep writing,
*   but people do not willingly read*

if they can find something else to amuse them—
*   every parent can conceive the fun*
of abusing a child. . . . no book is needed.

*   You cannot call such misers as mine*
sinners—they are merely exaggerations
*   of our mutual weakness, for they*

still cannot believe they own what they covet.
*   Sin is supposing we can possess*
our passions . . . Suppose we try another now:

I understand, hearing you speak so,
    that all human knowledge is guilty knowledge,
        and the only consequence is flight!

Eyes here, so! And afterwards . . . *Afterwards*
    you will sell me the plate. I must own it:
I must have myself. Nadar, the going rate?

Eugène Delacroix

Moorish Conversation, 1832

watercolor on paper, 5 × 7 inches,
The Metropolitan Museum of Art,
Ittelson Purchase Fund, 1963

Don't look now (I said *don't look!*
I'll tell you when you can look), just lie back
　　as if we were—well, as if
　we were *talking*. Try to behave
　as if we were by ourselves,
that's why I brought you here in the first place.
　　The trouble with these rooftop
　refuges—the one place in Tangier
　you can see a touch of green,
something alive besides men and camels—
　　the trouble is, there's always
　a roof higher than the one you're on,
　　a man looking down, watching . . .

　　Why bother getting really
comfortable if someone's . . . *In any case*
　　I'd never *dream* of dragging
　my best Bokhara out here—this old
　　Ardabil is lovely still,
they never lose their . . . The colors are fixed
　　by making the camels piss
　all over them, then washing them out
　　in the canal: harsh treatment,
you'd think, but it works—look at *me!*
　　all the suppler for the way
　I've been manhandled, you must admit . . .
　　Now look: you see what I mean?

That's a *man* up there, standing
where he can . . . No, not Mustapha! someone
he's *put* there to spy on us.
On *me*! What does it matter to *him*
whether I'm up here with you
or one of the bath-women? He has to
know, that's all, it affords him
some kind of gratification (more
than he gets from anything
he ever does with me!) . . . Try some of this,
she put the rose-petals in
just this morning, it tastes really fresh . . .
Oh! now I see: that . . . *person*

is nothing like Mustapha's
usual parasites. One thing I *do* have
is a good memory for
men's bodies. You must have noticed him:
a sharp-faced foreign devil
always lurking somewhere and *staring* so?
He takes it all in as if
life were *the scene of the crime*, even
the pair of *us*, harmless enough
on these irreproachable hassocks. Look!
I know he's the one, crouching
with a notebook in his artful hands:
he's put us in his picture!

As far as art goes—and art
such as his goes far enough for spying:
you don't suppose Mustapha
sold rights to the roof?—we incarnate
your typical Tangerine
dalliance. Can't you just hear the giddy

little screams once he returns
to his studio: "My dear, how
positively *classical!*" . . .
Never mind, he's leaving now. Some more
fresh *loukoum?* The tea's still warm,
and so am I. Do just as you like.
Mustapha might as well be blind!

Among the Missing

Know me? I am the ghost of Gansevoort Pier.
    Out of the Trucks, beside the garbage scow
    where rotten pilings form a sort of prow,
I loom, your practiced shadow, waiting here

for celebrants who cease to come my way,
    though mine are limbs as versatile as theirs
    and eyes as vagrant. Odd that no one cares
to ogle me now where I, as ever, lay

myself out, all my assets and then some,
    weather permitting. Is my voice so faint?
    Can't you hear me over the river's complaint?
Too dark to see me? Have you all become

ghosts? What earthly good is that? I want
    incarnate lovers hungry for my parts,
    longing hands and long-since-lonely hearts!
It is your living bodies I must haunt,

and while the Hudson hauls its burdens past,
    having no hosts to welcome or repel
    disclosures of the kind I do so well,
I with the other ghosts am laid at last.

Our Spring Trip

Dear Mrs. Masters, Hi from the Fifth-Grade Class
of Park School! We're still here in New York City
                        at the Taft Hotel,
you could have guessed that from the picture printed
on this stationery—I inked in x's
        to show you our rooms,
which are actually on the same floor as
the Terminal Tower Observation Deck
                        in Cleveland, Ohio,
which we visited on our *Fourth*-Grade Spring Trip,
but nowhere near so high as some skyscrapers
        in New York City:
we've been up to the *top* of the Empire State
and the Chrysler Buildings, which are really tall!
                        But there's another
reason for writing besides wanting to say
Hi—we're having a problem Miss Husband thought
        you might help us with,
once we get back to school . . . yesterday we went
to the Dinosaur Hall of the Natural
                        History Museum
for our Class Project—as you know, the Fifth Grade
is constructing this life-size Diplodocus
        out of chicken wire
and some stuff Miss Husband calls papier-mâché,
but no diagram we have shows how the tail
                        balances the head
to keep our big guy upright—we need to see
how the backbone of a real Diplodocus
        manages to bear

so much weight: did you know that some Dinosaurs
(like the Brontosaurus) are so huge they have
                              a whole other brain
at the base of their spine, just to move their tail?
Another thing: each time Arthur Englander
        came anywhere near
our Diplodocus, it would collapse because
of not balancing right. This went on until
                              David Stashower
got so mad at Arthur that he flew at him
and gave his left shoulder a really good bite
        so he would keep away . . .
That was when you called the All-School Assembly
to explain about the biting: biting's no good . . .
                              Even so, Arthur
decided not to come on this year's Spring Trip.
Well, we took a Subway train to the Museum
        from the Taft Hotel,
in fact that was our very first excursion,
but the noise, once we were on the platform,
                              was so loud one girl,
Nancy Akers, cried (she always was chicken)
when someone told her that terrible roaring
        the Expresses made
was Tyrannosaurus Rex himself, and she
believed it!—then we went to the Great Hall where
                              we were surrounded
by Dinosaurs, all the kinds we had studied:
some were not much bigger than a chicken, but
        some were humongous!
One was just a skeleton wired together,
so it was easy to see how we could make
                              our Diplodocus

balance by putting a swivel in its neck.
All the other Dinosaurs were stuffed, I guess,
     with motors and lights
inside: when they moved, *their* heads balanced their tails!
There was even a Pterodactyl flying
                         back and forth above
our heads, probably on some kind of a track.
But even though Miss Husband tried explaining
     (for the hundredth time)
how the Dinosaurs had all been extinct for
millions of years, not one person in the class
                         believed what she said:
the idea of a million years is so *stupid*,
anyway—a typical grown-up reason . . .

     You know the Klein twins,
the biggest brains in the whole Fifth Grade (a lot
bigger, probably, than *both* brains combined in
                         that Brontosaurus)—
well, they had a question for Miss Husband: what
if the Dinosaurs' being extinct so long
     was just a smoke screen
for their being Somewhere Else, a long ways away?
And Lucy Wensley made an awful pun on
                         stinky and *extinct* . . .
Actually, Mrs. Masters, we've already
figured it out, about death: the Dinosaurs
     may be extinct, but
they're not dead! It's a different thing, you dig?
When Duncan Chu's Lhasa jumped out the window,
                         or when Miss Husband's
parents were killed together in a car crash,
we understood that—that *was* being dead; gone:
     no body around.

Isn't that what dying has to mean—not being
here? The Dinosaurs are with us all the time,
                              anything but dead—
we keep having them! Later, at the "Diner-
Saurus," the Museum restaurant, there was
        chicken-breast for lunch
stamped out in the shape of a Triceratops!
Strange how everything has to taste like chicken:
                              whether it's rabbit
or rattlesnake, it's always "just like chicken" . . .
Anyway, Dinosaurs are alive as long
        as we think they are,
not like Duncan's dog. And that's just the problem.
By next week, though, we'll be back in Sandusky,
                              and while we're putting
the swivel into our Diplodocus's neck,
you could explain to us about Time—about
        those millions of years,
and Dinosaur-chicken in the Diner, and
chicken-size Dinosaurs in the Great Hall, and
                              where they really are.

Henri Fantin-Latour
Un Coin de table, 1873

All those men have gone. Over a year
since they left the table where you have arranged
   matters, assortment of properties
that set the "natural" stage of *natures mortes,*
   the apparatus of your practiced
art, or at the very least the articles
   of your everlasting apprenticeship:

the consuetudinal cup and glass,
the former drained to show your skill, the latter
   filled, for the same purpose, with wine from
a pitcher that has perdured here eighteen months
   (though turned, now, to face the other way);
a cruet which is well rehearsed, a compote
   covertly upstaged by that silver bowl . . .

You have shifted the rhododendrons
from the right (where they supplanted old Mérat
   who would not share a purposed *Hommage*
à Baudelaire with beasts of such behavior
   as the poets who stare in separate
lethargies past each other on the left:
   Rimbaud, Verlaine, abominable pair!)

to the foreground, lavish corollas
standing in for laureates of shameful life
   and for enshrined (and shaggy) lions
blameless in their oblivion ever since—
   now we name them only from the list
drawn up by the orderly Mlle Dubourg,
   whom you would marry in a few more years.

It was to maintain the new ménage
that you sold, in England, eight hundred portraits
    of flowers! while sending to the Salon
voluted *fantaisies* that have duly turned
    to more hectares of blackened leather
than all the Wagnerites in Paris could buy.
    You kept your shameful secret (so you thought)

    of those remunerative roses,
hollyhocks, pansies, peonies, whatever
    she brought in from the garden each day,
and went on portraying *ces messieurs* in all
    their grave coats, their cretacious collars,
their gold watch fobs and their contemptuous stares:
    "Around the Piano," "In a Batignolles

Studio"—and all the while you knew
what you dared to acknowledge only in oils:
    these perennials and the power
to paint air around them which was all you had,
    all you needed. At the retrospective
of '06, *tout-Paris* was fluttered to find
    such flowers never seen in France before.

    No lions here, and no Rhinemaidens,
just an empty table, its white cloth still creased,
    these months, as if fresh from the mangle,
the patient props and, wholly unjustified
    by any important theme or scheme,
not even a pot to grow in, these branches
    of rhododendron . . . This life . . . This art . . .

At 65

The tragedy, Colette said, is that one
does *not* age. Everyone else does, of course
(as Marcel was so shocked to discover),
and upon one's mask odd disfigurements
are imposed; but that garrulous presence
we sometimes call the self, sometimes deny

it exists at all despite its carping
monologue, is the same as when we stole
the pears, spied on mother in the bath, ran
away from home. What has altered is what
Kant called Categories: the shape of *time*
changes altogether! Days, weeks, months,

and especially years are reassigned.
Famous for her timing, a Broadway wit
told me her "method": asked to do something,
anything, she would acquiesce *next year*—
"I'll commit suicide, provided it's
next year." But after sixty-five, next year

is now. Hours? there are none, only a few
reckless postponements before *it is time* . . .
When was it you "last" saw Jimmy—last spring?
last winter? That scribbled arbiter
your calendar reveals—betrays—the date:
over a year ago. Come again? No

time like the present, endlessly deferred.
Which makes a difference: once upon a time
there was only time (. . . *as the day is long*)

between the wanting self and what it wants.
Wanting still, you have no dimension where
fulfillment or frustration can occur.

Of course you have, but you must cease waiting
upon it: simply turn around and look
back. Like Orpheus, like Mrs. Lot, you
will be petrified—astonished—to learn
memory is endless, life very long,
and you—you are immortal after all.